WORLD ENERGY ISSUES

SOLAR POWER
Energy for Free?

JIM PIPE

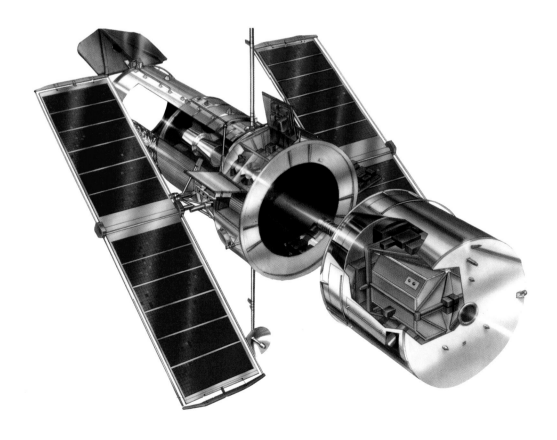

ALADDIN/WATTS
LONDON • SYDNEY

Contents

© Aladdin Books Ltd 2010

Designed and produced by
Aladdin Books Ltd
PO Box 53987
London SW15 2SF

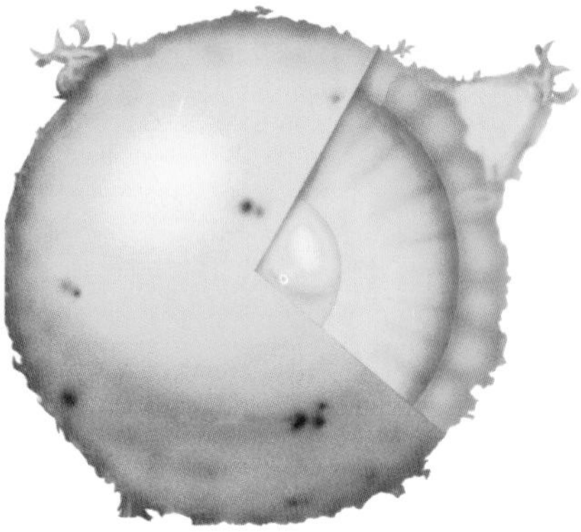

First published in 2010
by Franklin Watts
338 Euston Road
London NW1 3BH

Franklin Watts Australia
Level 17/207 Kent Street
Sydney NSW 2000

Franklin Watts is a division of
Hachette Children's Books,
an Hachette UK company.
www.hachette.co.uk

All rights reserved
Printed in Malaysia

Scientific consultant: Rob Bowden

A catalogue record for
this book is available
from the British Library.

Dewey Classification:
333.7'923

ISBN 978 1 4451 0193 4

What's the Issue?

Solar power is turning the Sun's energy into electricity or using it to heat buildings or water pipes. Though they may never provide enough energy for all our needs, the giant solar farms and solar heating systems being developed today could one day be a vital energy source alongside biofuels, wind, water and nuclear power.

Most of our energy today comes from oil, gas and coal. When they are burnt, these fossil fuels release gases that add to global warming, as well as polluting the air. Solar power is a clean source of energy, and unlike oil and gas supplies, it won't run out for billions of years. So the race is now on to find cheaper ways of trapping the Sun's energy and storing it. Today, solar power supplies only just 0.1 per cent of the world's energy, but some experts predict this could rise to 16 per cent by 2040.

◑ Solar farm – *Mirrors focus sunlight onto a tower. The superhot temperatures created boil water into steam, driving turbines that generate electricity.*

▽ Instant Power
This mat converts the Sun's heat energy into electricity to power an MP3 player.

Why Go Solar?

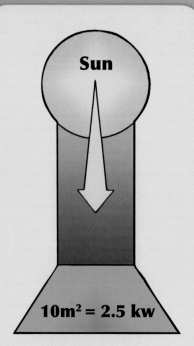

Sun

$10m^2 = 2.5$ kw

ENERGY FACTS: How Much Power?

On a sunny day you can really feel the heat of the Sun. Even so, in one day an area around 10 m² only receives the heat energy equivalent to the power used by an electric kettle (2.5 kilowatts). So if solar power was going to supply the world's energy needs, we would need to cover an area 500,000 km² in solar panels, roughly the size of Spain, or 1/18th the size of the Sahara (see page 27).

Solar power is the energy obtained from the rays of the Sun. The Sun's heat can be used directly to heat up water, cook food and warm buildings. Solar thermal engines use this heat to boil water into steam, powering turbines that generate electricity. Meanwhile, photovoltaic (PV) solar cells convert the energy in the Sun's rays directly into electricity.

The amount of solar energy reaching the Earth each minute is greater than the energy the world uses in fossil fuels each year. It's clean, renewable, and can be used locally. In the past, however, solar power systems were expensive and unreliable. Today, new technology is bringing down the cost. Linking solar power with wind turbines and hydroelectric dams could also create a reliable supply of electricity day and night.

It's Everywhere!

One advantage of solar power is that the Sun shines everywhere, though areas close to the Equator receive far more Sun than those close to the North or South Pole. By putting solar panels on top of houses, no extra land space is needed and unlike nuclear, oil or coal-fired power stations, there is no danger from pollution.

◗ Solar Cells

Solar cells trap sunlight and convert it into electricity. They work best in places where the Sun shines all year round.

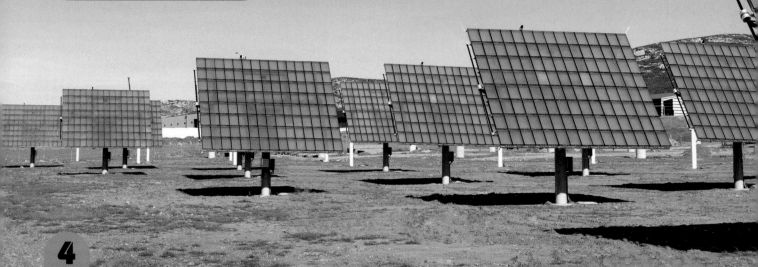

SOLAR POWER: For

• Solar power is renewable as the Sun is going to keep on shining for billions of years.

• Using solar power to generate electricity doesn't pollute or create the greenhouse gases that add to global warming.

• Solar power systems aren't noisy, unlike wind turbines.

• Once solar cells are put in place, they provide free energy. They have no moving parts that can get worn out.

• Solar power can provide electricity in remote areas where buildings are not connected to the grid – even in space.

• Buildings that capture the Sun's heat are a cheap and effective form of solar energy.

SOLAR POWER: Against

• Solar cells are expensive to produce as the material they are made from, silicon, is hard to dig out of the ground and purify.

• It takes four years to create enough energy from one solar cell to make up for the amount of energy used to make it.

• The Sun does not shine at night, so solar energy is not a reliable source of energy without finding a cheap and effective way to store the energy (batteries are expensive).

• It would take a very large solar farm to provide the same power as a coal-fired or nuclear power station.

• Solar (PV) panels don't work well in cloudy areas or where the air is heavily polluted.

Solar Power Systems

♉ Active Heating – *Heat energy from the Sun can be used to heat water for homes or swimming pools. Most systems are mounted on roofs and use glass to trap the Sun's heat.*

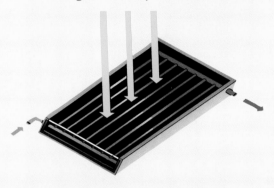

♉ Solar Thermal Engines *use curved mirrors to focus the Sun's energy onto a small area, creating high enough temperatures to boil water into steam. This drives turbines that generate electricity.*

♉ Passive Heating – *Sunlight is used to warm and light a building, using glass to trap the heat inside.*

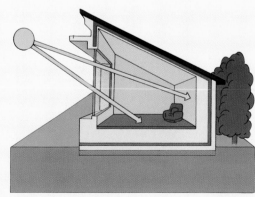

What Is Solar Energy?

The Sun, a huge burning ball of gas, is our nearest star. Like other stars, it is powered by a process known as nuclear fusion. At the Sun's core, the high temperatures (15 million °C) and the massive force of gravity cause hydrogen atoms to turn into helium atoms.

These reactions create enormous amounts of energy. This flows to the surface of the Sun and then travels out into space in all directions. On Earth, the mixture of heat, light and other rays from the Sun can be used to heat water and generate electricity – what we call solar energy.

◐ Burning Fireball

The Sun's heat and light are caused by a giant nuclear reaction inside the Sun's core.

▽ How Fusion Creates Solar Energy

▽ Fusion

At the Sun's core, hydrogen atoms come together to form helium atoms and vast amounts of energy. The hydrogen atoms come in two different forms, or isotopes, called deuterium and tritium. The extra neutrons they contain (compared to the ordinary hydrogen atoms found in water) are also released during fusion.

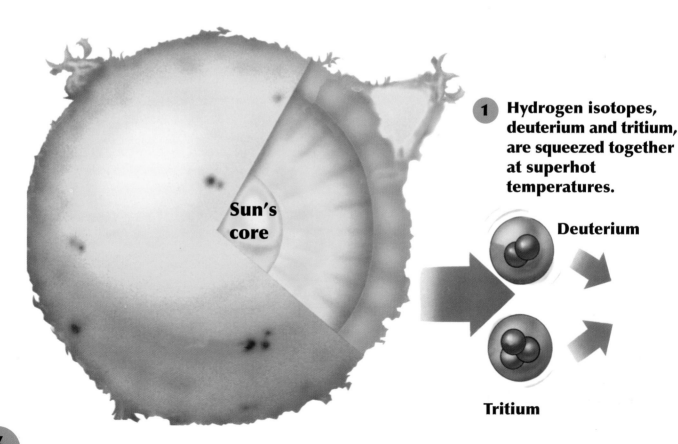

Sun's core

1 Hydrogen isotopes, deuterium and tritium, are squeezed together at superhot temperatures.

Deuterium

Tritium

Sun

♻ Our Energy Source

In different ways, the Sun provides almost all of our energy. It warms our planet, creating the weather systems that cause wind and waves – two forms of renewable energy. This weather also creates rain, filling the reservoirs that dams use to produce hydroelectric power.

We also release the Sun's energy when we burn fossil fuels. These are the remains of ancient plants and animals that stored the Sun's energy as carbon in their leaves or bodies.

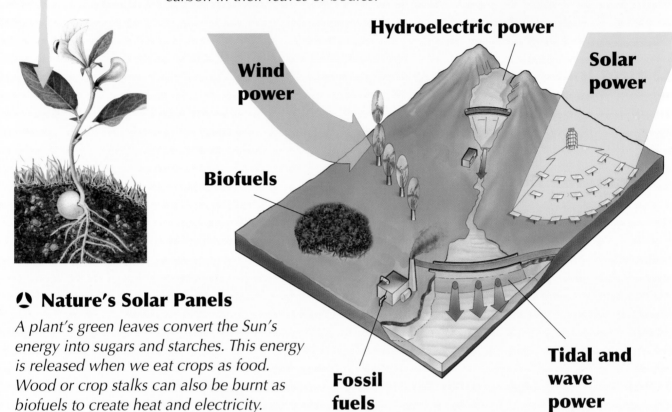

Hydroelectric power

Wind power

Solar power

Biofuels

Fossil fuels

Tidal and wave power

♻ Nature's Solar Panels

A plant's green leaves convert the Sun's energy into sugars and starches. This energy is released when we eat crops as food. Wood or crop stalks can also be burnt as biofuels to create heat and electricity.

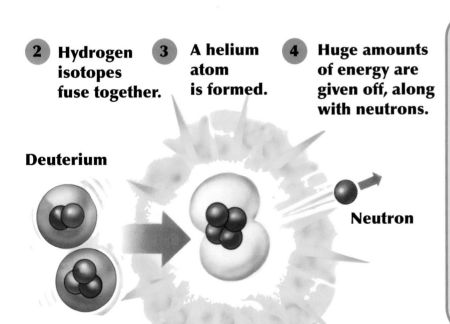

2 Hydrogen isotopes fuse together.

3 A helium atom is formed.

4 Huge amounts of energy are given off, along with neutrons.

Deuterium

Neutron

Tritium

ENERGY FACTS: Invisible Energy

The Sun also gives off its energy as invisible electrical and magnetic waves, such as infrared waves, radio waves and X-rays. Invisible ultraviolet (UV) rays from the Sun can burn your skin if it is exposed for too long. All these rays travel through space at the speed of light, nearly 300,000 km per second, travelling the 150 million km from the Sun to the Earth in just 8 minutes.

Passive Heating

⚠ Heat Trap
When windows face south, they catch the Sun's rays all day long.

There are many ways of capturing the heat energy from the Sun. To create passive heating, buildings are designed to face the Sun and trap solar energy using glass and other materials.

In active heating, special collectors soak up the Sun's rays and use them to heat water for hot baths and showers, and for swimming pools. These collectors also use glass to trap the heat and are usually mounted on roofs. In hot countries, water is simply run through a flat box exposed to the Sun.

✪ Trapping the Sun's Heat

For thousands of years, people have used sunlight to warm and light their houses. Many modern houses are especially designed to use solar energy in this way. Glass traps the heat inside the building, then air circulates the energy around the house, usually without needing pumps or fans. The walls and floors are made from thick materials or have an insulating layer that holds in the heat. They keep the house warm at night when temperatures outside fall.

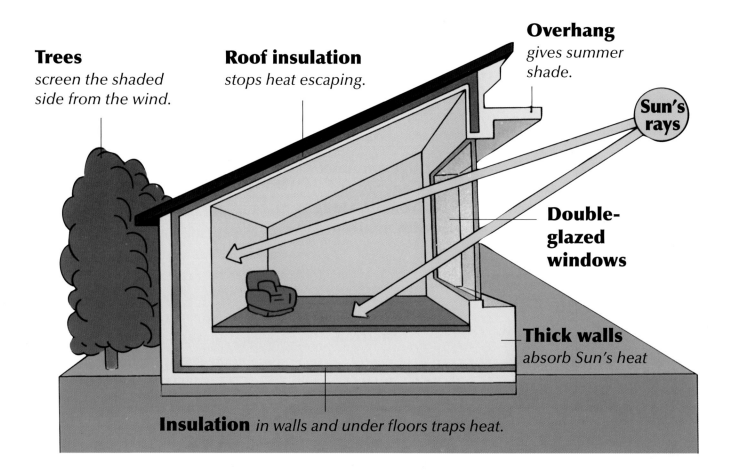

Overhang *gives summer shade.*

Trees *screen the shaded side from the wind.*

Roof insulation *stops heat escaping.*

Sun's rays

Double-glazed windows

Thick walls *absorb Sun's heat*

Insulation *in walls and under floors traps heat.*

Glass – A Magic Material

Both passive and active solar heating use glass. This amazing material allows light to pass through while blocking the wind and trapping heat inside. In recent years, manufacturers have found new ways of making glass as transparent as possible, while covering it with a special coating that helps to reflect heat back into the building.

Flat-bed collector

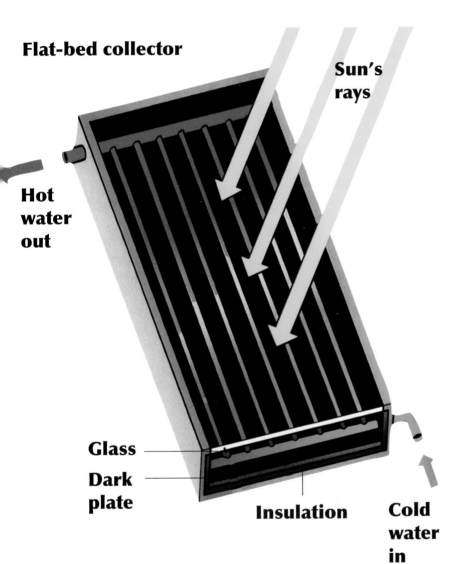

Sun's rays

Hot water out

Glass

Dark plate

Insulation

Cold water in

◑ Greenhouses

Gardeners use greenhouses to trap the Sun's heat and grow plants that need warm air to grow. The glass roof and walls let in the sunlight and trap its heat inside.

◑ Active Heating Collectors

Flat-bed collectors are made of a shallow metal box with a glass cover and a dark-coloured plate at the bottom, as dark surfaces absorb (soak up) the Sun's heat best. The glass traps heat that the dark plate absorbs. Water is then slowly pumped through pipes attached to the plate and gets warmed up.

The warm water flows into a heat exchanger, which transfers the heat and provides hot water for washing, cooking, heating rooms at night or swimming pools.

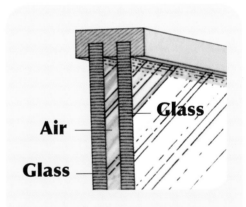

Glass

Air

Glass

◑ Why Two Layers?

Double-glazed windows have two panes of glass that trap the air between them. Because heat travels through the air much slower than it does through glass, a lot less heat is lost through the window. For even greater insulation, extra panes of glass are added and argon gas is put into the gap between the panels instead of air.

Solar Heating

Solar tubes

Pump

Tank

Gas boiler

Flat-bed collectors work very well in hot countries such as Israel, where 80 per cent of homes use solar heating. They have also been tested on a large scale in huge tanks known as solar ponds. However, a lot of the heat escapes, so in colder climates like that in the UK, more efficient collectors known as solar tubes are used. Sunny countries such as Greece and Saudi Arabia also use the Sun's heat to turn seawater into drinking water.

◐ How It Works

Solar tubes can provide all the hot water a house needs for 6 to 9 months of the year. The special fluid they heat up flows down to a water tank where it warms the water you actually use, like the electric coil in a kettle.

During the winter months, another coil at the top of the tank is heated by a gas or wood-pellet boiler, bringing the water up to the right temperature.

▼ Solar Tubes

Solar tubes consist of two tubes of strong glass. The outer tube is transparent, allowing sunlight to pass through. The inner tube has a dark coating that absorbs heat from the Sun and warms the fluid inside. This turns into a gas that rises to the top of the tube. Here it heats a pipe filled with more fluid, which is connected to the water tank. The tube can heat water even on very cold days (down to about -40 °C).

▼ Like A Thermos Flask

The air is pumped out of solar tubes, creating a vacuum like the one in a Thermos flask. Heat travels slowly through the vacuum, so 95 per cent of the Sun's heat gets in, but only 5 per cent escapes. Even when the temperature on the inside of the tube is 150 °C, the outer tube is cold to the touch.

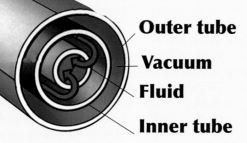

Outer tube

Vacuum

Fluid

Inner tube

⚆ From Salty To Fresh Water

A shortage of fresh water is a major problem in many less developed countries in Africa and Asia. In the future, small water treatment plants powered by the Sun could be used to transform salty seawater or brackish water from salt lakes into pure drinking water. The plants will use a special membrane that allows the steam from heated salt water to pass through and condense (turn to water), leaving the salt behind.

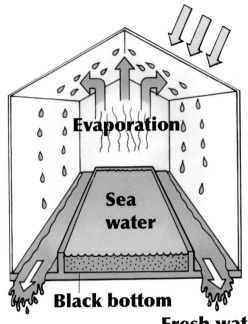

Evaporation

Sea water

Black bottom

Fresh water

Salt Lake, Tunisia

⚇ Solar Distillation Plant

Sea water is poured into tanks painted black to absorb the heat of the Sun. Sloping panes of glass are then placed on top.

The Sun's heat makes the water evaporate and it condenses on the glass, leaving the salt in the tank. Fresh water trickles down the glass panes into troughs and is then piped into another tank ready for use.

⚈ Solar Ponds

Solar ponds use the Sun's heat to create electricity. They have a bottom painted black to trap the Sun's heat. They are filled with salt water, which absorbs more heat from the Sun than fresh water.

How It Works

1 *The saltiest water drifts down to the bottom, where the temperature can reach 90 °C.*
2 *This hot water is pumped to a boiler where it heats up a separate tank of fresh water, turning it to steam.*
3 *The steam drives a turbine, generating electricity.*
4 *The steam is then cooled back to water by cold salt water from the pond.*

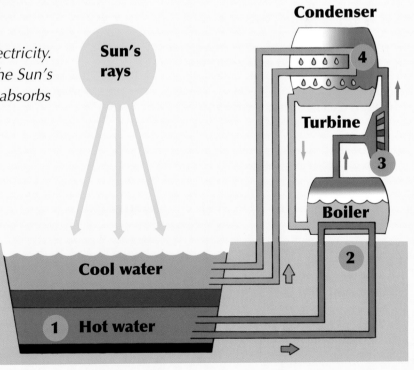

Condenser

Sun's rays

4

Turbine

3

Boiler

2

Cool water

1 Hot water

Superhot Collectors

We've seen how the Sun's heat can be used locally to provide hot water and drinking water. Solar collectors are also used on a giant scale to produce electricity. In solar farms, banks of mirrors focus the power of the Sun's rays onto a liquid such as molten salt, creating superhot temperatures that are used to boil water and turn it into steam. The hot steam pushes against turbines, producing electricity for homes and factories. In some power plants, these solar thermal engines work alongside generators that run on diesel oil to provide power day and night.

Concentrated Solar Power

The hotter they get, the more efficient solar collectors get. That's why mirrors are used to focus the Sun's power on one point, creating superhot temperatures.

This method is known as Concentrated Solar Power or CSP. A CSP plant can produce electricity day and night, as storing heat is much cheaper and more efficient than storing electricity.

▷ Power Troughs

Power troughs use curved mirrors to bounce sunlight onto thin steel pipes, heating the fluid inside to 390 ºC. This fluid is then piped to a heat exchanger. This boils water into steam, which is used to drive the turbines.

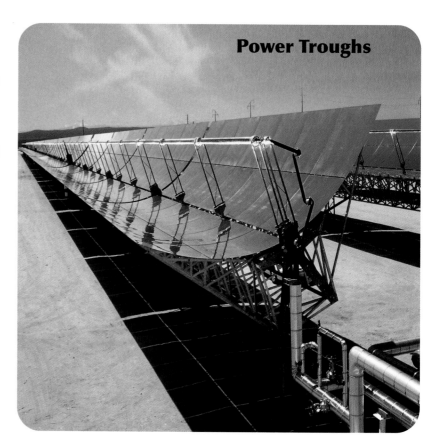

Power Troughs

▷ Tracking the Sun

By following the Sun's course across the sky, power troughs get the benefit of the Sun's direct rays all day long. The tracking motor can be solar-powered.

Morning

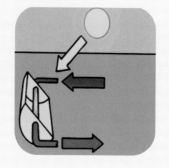

Midday

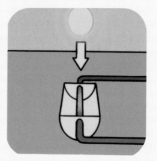

Afternoon

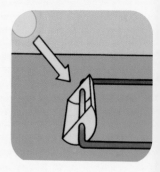

Solar Towers

There are plans to build a giant 150 MW solar tower near the city of Palm Springs, California that will provide power for 90,000 homes. Some 18,000 moving mirrors, or heliostats, will track the Sun as it moves across the sky. They will aim light at the 164-m-high tower, heating the salt inside to such great temperatures (up to 500 °C) that it melts. Heat from the salt is used to boil water into steam that spins a turbine. The heat can be released up to seven hours later, at night or when it is cloudy.

PS10 Solar Tower
The world's first commercial tower was built in 2007 in Almeria, Spain. In the future, it could provide enough power for the 600,000 inhabitants of the city of Seville.

Solar Furnace

How a Solar Furnace Works

1 *Banks of moving mirrors, or heliostats, reflect sunlight onto a large curved mirror.*
2 *The large mirror focuses all the Sun's rays on a collector, filled with liquid that keeps its heat for a long time.*
3 *The liquid is pumped into containers. When power is needed, the liquid flows to a heat exchanger where it heats water and produces steam to drive a turbine.*

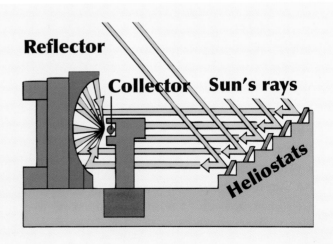

Reflector
Collector   Sun's rays
Heliostats

Solar Cells

We have looked at how solar energy can be used to turn water into steam to drive a turbine. In the 1960s, scientists developed solar cells that could capture the energy in the Sun's rays and turn it directly into electricity.

Made from tiny slivers of silicon coated with special chemicals, modern photovoltaic cells (PV) can turn more than 25 per cent of the sunlight that shines on them into electricity. Small solar cells commonly power watches and calculators. On solar farms, however, huge numbers of PV cells are grouped together in large panels that face the Sun.

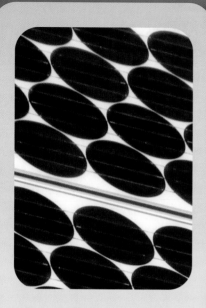

◑ Solar PV Cells

A group of solar cells is known as a solar panel. The cells are linked by an electrical circuit.

◐ PV Solar Farm

Over 100,000 solar panels are grouped together in a 35 MW solar farm, providing enough energy for 20,000 homes.

ENERGY FACTS: Powering a Home

In the UK, a typical house uses around 1,000 kilowatt hours of electricity a year for lighting and to power electrical appliances such as fridges, washing machines, TVs and computers. To supply all this with solar power alone, a solar panel around 9 m² in area would be needed on a roof facing south, where it would catch the Sun for most of the day.

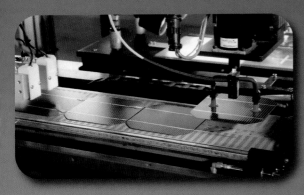

☀ Manufacturing PV Cells

Until recently, most solar cells were made from very pure silicon with almost no defects. The process to purify the silicon was complicated and expensive.

Scientific teams across the world are now looking into cheaper methods and materials, such as incredibly thin sheets of plastic stacked on top of each other, or tiny silicon spheres cased in aluminium foil.

How Solar Cells Work

When sunlight shines on a solar cell, the Sun's energy makes tiny particles called electrons jump around, creating electricity.

1 *The sunlight passes through the glass cover of the cell and hits atoms in two separate layers of silicon.*

2 *One layer, the n, or negative, layer collects electrons that jump from the p, or positive, layer.*

3 *When the electrons jump from one layer of silicon to another, electricity is created.*

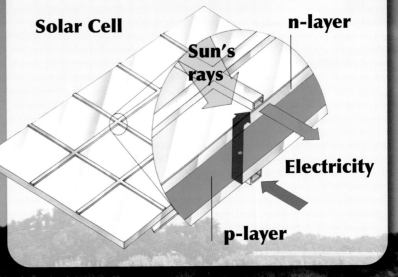

Solar Cell

n-layer

Sun's rays

Electricity

p-layer

Using PV Cells

☀ Solar Lighthouses

The US Coast Guard relies almost entirely on solar power for its buoys and lighthouses. In Australia, PV panels are used to power telephones in rural areas.

Solar cells can be used to power all sorts of gadgets, especially lightweight items that do not need much power, such as calculators. In these, PV cells are linked to rechargeable batteries. Roadside telephones, parking meters, flashing road signs and lights in bus shelters can all work on the power created by solar cells. Houses and flats can also use them to supply electricity.

Solar cells can provide power for transport without creating pollution, but only for light vehicles the size of golf carts, as there is limited space for solar cells on the roof. However, spare electricity from a much bigger array, such as on the roof of a house, could be used to charge an electric car during peak hours when the Sun is shining brightly.

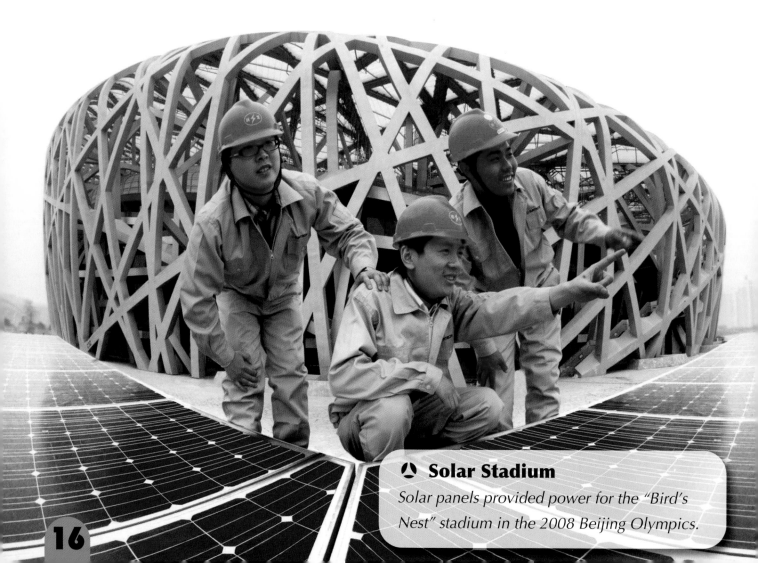

☀ Solar Stadium
Solar panels provided power for the "Bird's Nest" stadium in the 2008 Beijing Olympics.

▷ Helios

This plane can stay in the air a long time to study weather patterns. The power for its engines comes from solar panels on its wings.

Solar Transport

Scientists and engineers have adapted solar power for planes, cars and boats. The American Solar Challenge race of 2010 took place over 1,760 km in Oklahoma and Illinois, USA, running on nothing but sunshine. The winning car averaged a speed of over 74 km/h.

ENERGY FACTS:
Solar-Powered Record Breakers

1981 The *Solar Challenger* aircraft flew 280 km from France to England and reached a height of 3,300 m. It had over 16,000 solar cells mounted on its wings.

1996 Japanese sailor Kenichi Horie crossed the Pacific Ocean in a boat with a solar-powered engine.

1998 The *Pathfinder* remote-controlled solar plane flew to a record height of 24,000 m above sea level.

2001 The pilotless *Helios* (above) achieved a new height record of 29,524 m. Its 14 propellers were powered by 62,120 solar cells spread across the top of its 75-m wide wing.

2007-8 The solar-powered *Solartaxi* drove around the world. It covered 50,000 km in 18 months and crossed 40 countries.

Solar Lighting

Solar Parking Meters

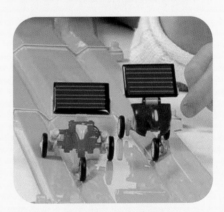

Solar-Powered Toys

Bags *that can power mobile phones or MP3 players*

Local Power

Though solar power works best in hot and sunny countries, new technology means it can work well even in colder regions. It has even been used to help power scientific bases in Antarctica and small towns in northern (Arctic) Canada. Solar power works well for people living in remote or less developed parts of the world where they are "off-grid", which means there are no electrical power lines or networks of gas or oil pipes to provide fuel.

◑ **Solar Towns** *are springing up all over the world. This housing estate in the city of Amersfoort in the Netherlands runs on electricity from rooftop solar cells. In Japan, 75 per cent of the houses in Pal Town (80 km northwest of Tokyo), have solar panels.*

More Developed Countries

Many European countries offer grants to encourage home owners to install solar panels on their roofs and sell spare electricity back to the grid. In Japan, the government aims to have solar power systems installed on more than 70 per cent of new homes, while in the United States the state of Massachusetts has set up a scheme that provides cheap solar panels for homeowners, schools and businesses.

▼ **Solar-Powered School**
The Star school in Arizona, USA, is completely powered by solar energy.

India's Solar Programme

In India, solar power is used to supply fresh drinking water and lighting to villages without mains electricity. By early 2009, more than 435,000 home lighting systems, 700,000 solar lanterns, 7,000 solar-powered water pumps and 635,000 solar cookers had been installed as part of India's Remote Village Electrification programme.

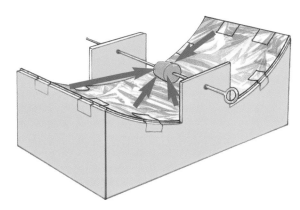

☀ Solar Cooker

The Sun's rays can be focused to create enough heat to cook food. This avoids the need to collect firewood for cooking, which can take many hours in areas far from woodland.

In a solar cooker, curved pieces of shiny metal reflect sunlight on to a small area, either an oven or a metal ring holding a pot or kettle. As the Sun moves, the solar cooker can be adjusted to best face it.

☀ Community Power in Africa

Solar power is ideally suited to many parts of Africa. This village (left) in Botswana runs on solar power, which provides electricity for street lighting and community buildings such as the school and medical centre. In Morocco, a German project completed in 2008 fitted some 40,000 households with PV panels.

☀ Solar Still

A new device, the Watercone, uses the Sun's heat to turn salt water into drinking water.

1 *You pour saltwater into the black pan.*

2 *The black pan absorbs the Sun's heat, making the water evaporate.*

3 *The evaporated water condenses on the inner wall of the cone and trickles down to the trough at the bottom.*

4 *You lift the cone off the black pan, unscrew the cap and tip out the fresh water.*

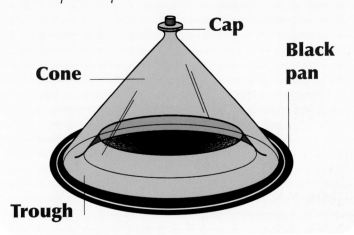

Cap — Black pan — Cone — Trough

Solar in Space

Solar cells can be used to power spacecraft. In space, the sunlight is more intense as there are no clouds or atmosphere to get in the way. Satellites have solar cells all the way round as they constantly rotate. These power on-board computers, cameras and radios. Larger craft, such as the Hubble space telescope, have flat panels that stick out like wings. Most solar panels can be pivoted as the spacecraft moves, so they always point towards the Sun.

◑ Solar Cells

Astronauts repairing a satellite in space. Note the solar panels wrapped around the outside of the satellite.

◔ International Space Station

The International Space Station that orbits up to 420 km above the Earth is powered by a large array of solar panels arranged into four pairs of wings.

Each array is about 375 m² in area and 58 m long. The solar arrays track the Sun to maximise the amount of solar power and have a total output of 110 kilowatts (kW).

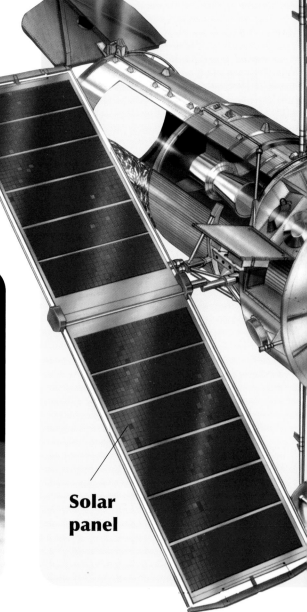

Solar panel

◄ Moon Collectors

Some scientists have suggested putting solar collectors on the Moon and some planets to trap the Sun's energy. This would create a ready supply of electricity for future space missions or colonies.

Others have proposed setting up a Lunar solar power station, which would beam power back to Earth using microwaves.

▼ Solar-Powered Rovers

In January 2004, two spacecraft landed on Mars containing the exploration rovers, *Spirit* and *Opportunity*. These were soon rolling across the Red Planet, sending amazing pictures back to Earth. The rovers were powered by solar panels that could generate up to 140 watts for up to four hours per Martian day, or "sol".

The power was stored in rechargeable batteries to provide energy at night. Though in July 2007, large dust storms blocked the sunlight, the rovers were back in action once the storms lifted.

Hubble Space Telescope

Each wing on the space telescope has a solar cell blanket that generates 2.8 kilowatts (kW) of electricity. Some of the energy is stored in on-board batteries so Hubble can operate while it's in Earth's shadow (which is about 36 minutes out of each 97-minute orbit).

Telescope

The Solar Revolution

Solar power is one of the fastest growing industries in the world. In 2000, almost 90 per cent of the world's solar-generated electricity was produced at the Kramer Junction plant in the Mojave desert in California, USA. Now large solar farms (left) are being built all over the world and dozens more are planned.

Solar power has the potential to generate 15,000 MW of energy in a few years' time – enough to power over 10 million homes. Rapid innovation means that the next generation of solar cells will capture far more energy and cost a lot less than they do today.

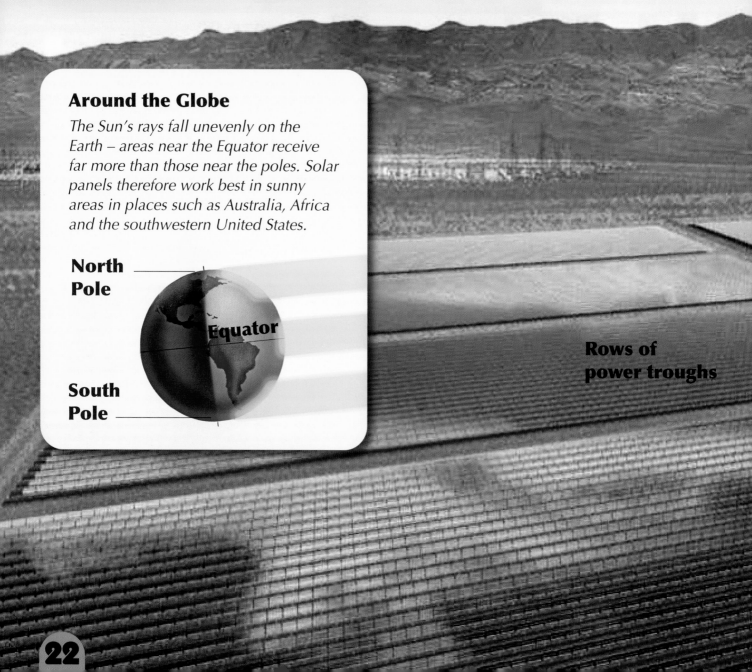

Around the Globe

The Sun's rays fall unevenly on the Earth – areas near the Equator receive far more than those near the poles. Solar panels therefore work best in sunny areas in places such as Australia, Africa and the southwestern United States.

North Pole

Equator

South Pole

Rows of power troughs

A Thirsty Industry

Solar farms take up a lot of space, so they work best in desert areas near to large cities. However, a large farm also uses billions of litres of water for cooling in these dry areas where water is scarce. As a result, plans for some solar farms have been turned down due to opposition from local farmers and wildlife groups over water supplies.

⊽ Solar One

This 10 MW solar farm in Nevada, USA uses power troughs to turn the Sun's heat into electricity using turbines. Such farms will become an increasingly common sight in sunny countries.

Storing Solar Power

Storing electricity can be difficult but heat can be stored more easily. Water hot enough for use in homes and offices can be stored by turning it into high pressure steam. Steam generators can store heat for up to 16 hours – long enough to last overnight. Solar energy can be stored cheaply at high temperatures using molten salts, as shown by test solar towers built in the 1990s.

Scientists are also looking at using solar power to produce the hydrogen gas that is used in fuel cells. In the future, these may be widely used to power cars and buildings.

Turbines

Cooling towers

ENERGY FACTS: The Biggest Solar Farm?

In recent years, new solar farms have competed to become the "world's biggest".

- Pöcking, Germany – 10 MW
- Serpa, Portugal – 11 MW
- Bavaria, Germany – 12 MW
- Nevada, USA – 18 MW
- Beneixama, Spain – 20 MW
- Saxony, Germany – 40 MW
- Olmedilla, Spain – 60 MW

Solar plants are set to get even bigger, however, with plans for solar farms in:

- Brandis, Germany – 80 MW
- Dunhuang City, China – 100 MW
- Negev Desert, Israel – 100 MW
- New Mexico, USA – 300 MW

One megawatt (MW) of electricity supplies enough power for around 600 typical European homes.

Future Trends

Superthin Panels

Power Plastic is a very thin PV material that captures both indoor and outdoor light and converts it into electricity. It can be built into all sorts of products.

The future of solar power is looking bright! A wave of new companies aim to revolutionise the world of solar power, with solar panels being replaced by solar cells sprayed onto walls and roads or built into windows and roof tiles.

Other projects include enormous solar power towers, solar dishes and even plans to beam solar power down from giant space satellites using microwaves.

◖ Satellite Power

A lot of solar energy is lost on its way through the Earth's atmosphere. One way to avoid this is to build a giant solar power collector in space.

There are several plans to do this by 2030. The satellite could beam the power back to Earth using laser beams or microwaves. It would remain in a fixed position so the Sun would shine on it for 99 per cent of the time.

◖ Smart Grids, Intelligent Buildings

In the future, smart grids will allow spare electricity generated by homeowners or farmers to be sold to the grid. PV panels will then supply electricity directly into the national network, working alongside power stations or wind farms. Meanwhile intelligent building technology will control heating and lighting systems more closely, saving electricity.

◖ Power Dish

One innovation is a solar dish that focuses the Sun's heat on a small generator. It works like a small solar furnace (page 13).

Spray-on Solar Cells

Several firms around the world are working to develop liquid-plastic solar cells that can be sprayed or painted onto buildings, cars, windows or roads. Some are using ultra-small solar cells that measure less than $\frac{1}{4}$ the size of a grain of rice. Others are designing solar cells with a rough surface that will absorb more sunlight.

◖ Solar Chimney

In 1981, a solar chimney power plant was built near Manzanares, 150 km south of Spain's capital, Madrid. It was surrounded by a huge circular greenhouse. Cool air entered the greenhouse from the sides and was heated by the Sun's rays. The warm air rose and rushed up the tower at over 50 km/h. The moving air drove wind turbines linked to generators producing electricity. Though the Manzanares project is finished, a solar power tower is planned in Australia that will be 990 m tall. This could one day generate electricity for 200,000 homes.

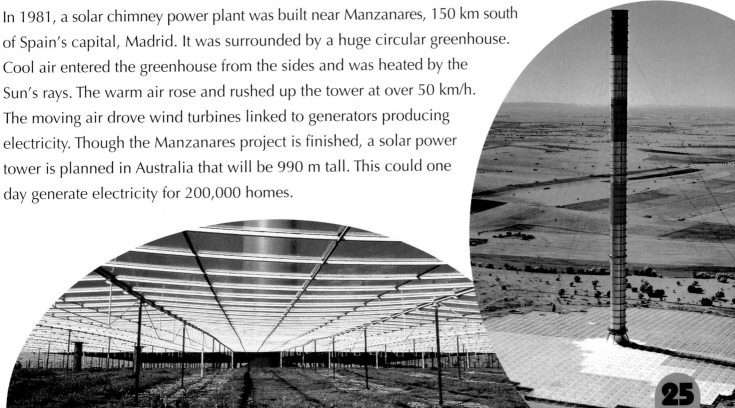

HOT OFF THE PRESS

Solar sail on *IKAROS* spacecraft

Solar Spaceship

■ On 21 May 2010, JAXA, the Japanese Aerospace Exploration agency, successfully launched the world's first fully-solar powered spacecraft into orbit. The craft is named *IKAROS*, after the youth in Greek mythology who flew too close to the Sun.

IKAROS' giant solar sail, 20 m across, is covered with a thin film of solar cells to generate electricity. The spacecraft will spend six months travelling to Venus, and then will begin a three-year journey to the far side of the Sun.

Around the World

■ The world's largest solar powered ship, *PlanetSolar*, was launched in 2010. It has up to 500 m² of PV solar panels. These can provide enough power to reach an average speed of 8 knots (15 km/h), with a top speed twice that. There are plans to sail the ship around the world.

Solar "Trees" provide shade and electricity.

Solar Trees

■ One new idea is "solar trees" for school playgrounds – these giant shades look like patio umbrellas, but have solar panels on top.

The umbrellas spin, so they can be adjusted to catch the Sun at any angle. They also serve as shade for the children to play under, perfect for a hot climate like Australia. The idea could also be adapted to provide shade for parked cars.

PlanetSolar, the world's largest solar-powered ship

Harnessing the Heat of the Sahara

■ A group of solar power firms aim to supply Europe with 15 per cent of its energy needs by 2050. Project Desertec plans to create a vast network of solar power plants, wind farms and power grids stretching 17,000 km^2 across North Africa and the Middle East.

The first stage will be to build massive solar energy fields across North Africa's Sahara desert. These will use curved mirrors to focus the Sun's rays on containers of water. The super-heated water will power steam turbines, generating electricity 24 hours a day, all year round. The electricity will then be transported under the Mediterranean Sea to Europe using hi-tech cables designed to reduce the amount of power lost in transmission.

More energy falls on the world's deserts in six hours than the world consumes in a year!

Organic Solar Cells Operate in Low Light

■ Teams of scientists across the world are developing organic PV cells that contain carbon. In the future, such cells could combine high power output while being much cheaper than today's silicon PV cells.

These cells produce electricity even in very low light and indoor conditions, opening up a whole range of new applications. The materials are ultra-thin and very flexible. The transparent solar cells can also be laid on top of windows, creating power-generating glass.

❝ Organic PV cells can even harvest power in the dark – from infra-red light that we can't see! **❞**

Solar sail

Combining Solar and Wind Power

■ An Australian firm has come up with a design that combines solar and wind power in a solar sail. The wings move automatically, tracking the Sun to create the best balance of solar power and wind power. In extremely windy conditions, the sails fold down against the boat.

Jumbo jet sized solar-powered sails have also been designed for cargo ships. These could reduce fuel costs by around 30 per cent as well as supplying some of the on-board electricity.

27

How Solar Compares

While fossil fuels are cheap, they release carbon dioxide into the atmosphere, causing global warming. Solar power and other forms of renewable energy will reduce this problem, but may only be able to supply 20 per cent of our energy needs by 2025. Nuclear power could provide us with the extra power, but reactors are very expensive and take years to build.

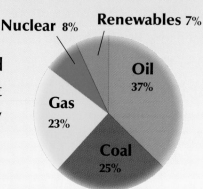

World Energy Sources

Nuclear 8% Renewables 7% Oil 37% Gas 23% Coal 25%

NON-RENEWABLE ENERGY

Oil

For:
Oil is cheap and easy to store, transport and use.

Against:
Oil is not renewable and it is getting more expensive to get out of the ground. Burning oil releases large amounts of greenhouse gases. Oil spills, especially at sea, cause severe pollution.

Gas

For:
Gas is relatively cheap, and produces less greenhouses gases than oil and coal.

Against:
Burning gas releases carbon dioxide. Gas is not renewable and the world's natural gas reserves are limited. Gas pipelines can disrupt the migration routes of animals such as caribou.

Coal

For:
Coal is cheap and supplies of coal are expected to last another 150 years.

Against:
Coal-fired power stations give off the most greenhouse gases. They also produce sulphur dioxide, creating acid rain. Coal mining can be very destructive to the landscape.

Nuclear

For:
Nuclear power is constant and reliable, and doesn't contribute to global warming.

Against:
Not renewable as uranium (the main nuclear fuel) will eventually run out. Nuclear waste is so dangerous it must be buried for thousands of years. Also the risk of a nuclear accident.

RENEWABLE ENERGY

Solar Power

For:
Solar power needs no fuel, it's renewable and doesn't pollute.

Against:
Solar farms using PV cells are still relatively expensive – they cost a lot to make compared to the amount of electricity they produce. They're unreliable unless used in a very sunny climate.

Wind Power

For:
Wind power needs no fuel, it's renewable and doesn't pollute.

Against:
Wind is unpredictable, so wind farms need a back-up power supply. Possible danger to bird flocks. It takes thousands of wind turbines to produce the same power as a nuclear plant.

Hydroelectric Power

For:
Hydroelectric power needs no fuel, is renewable and doesn't pollute.

Against:
Hydro-electric is very expensive to build. A big dam floods a very large area upstream, impacting on animals and people there. The flooded areas give off methane, a greenhouse gas.

Geothermal Power

For:
Geothermal power needs no fuel, it's renewable and doesn't pollute.

Against:
There aren't many suitable places for a geothermal power station as you need hot rocks of the right type and not too deep. It can "run out of steam". Underground poisonous gases can be a danger.

Biofuels

For:
Biofuels are cheap and renewable and can be made from waste.

Against:
Growing biofuels from energy crops reduces the land available for food and uses up vital resources such as fresh water. Like fossil fuels, biofuels can produce greenhouse gases.

Tidal Power

For:
Tidal power needs no fuel, is reliable, renewable and doesn't pollute.

Against:
Tidal power machines are expensive to build and only provide power for around 10 hours each day, when the tide is actually moving in or out. Not an efficient way of producing electricity.

Glossary and Resources

active heating Collecting the Sun's heat energy and using it to heat water for hot baths, showers and swimming pools.

atmosphere The thick blanket of air that surrounds the Earth.

climate The average weather in a region over a long period of time.

double-glazing Windows with two panes of glass that trap the air between them, reducing the amount of heat lost.

fossil fuel A fuel such as coal, oil or gas that is formed underground from the remains of prehistoric plants and animals.

fusion When two atoms join together, which releases large amounts of energy.

generator A machine that turns mechanical energy into electrical energy.

global warming A warming of the Earth's surface. Many scientists predict that global warming may lead to more floods, droughts and rising sea levels.

greenhouse effect The global warming caused by human-made gases, such as carbon dioxide and methane, which trap the heat from the Sun in the atmosphere.

heliostat A moveable mirror that tracks the Sun and reflects sunlight.

megawatt (MW) A million watts (a watt is a unit of power). A gigawatt is 1,000 MW.

nucleus The central part of an atom.

passive heating Using sunlight to warm and light a building, often using glass to trap the heat inside.

photovoltaic (PV) cell A solar cell that turns sunlight directly into electricity.

power station A plant where electricity is generated.

pylon A tall metal tower that supports high voltage electric cables.

radiation Energy given out in waves by high-energy particles. The Sun's radiation includes light rays and infrared heat waves.

renewable Something that can be used over and over without running out.

solar chimney A tall tower in which warm air heated by the Sun turns wind turbines to generate electricity.

solar collector A device that traps the Sun's heat.

solar furnace A power plant that uses mirrors to focus the Sun's heat, boiling water into steam that drives a turbine.

solar pond A large saltwater pond that uses the Sun's heat to turn water into steam and drive a turbine.

solar tubes A solar heating system made up of two glass tubes. The dark inner tube absorbs heat from the Sun and transfers it to a hot water system using a special fluid.

turbine A machine with rotating blades.

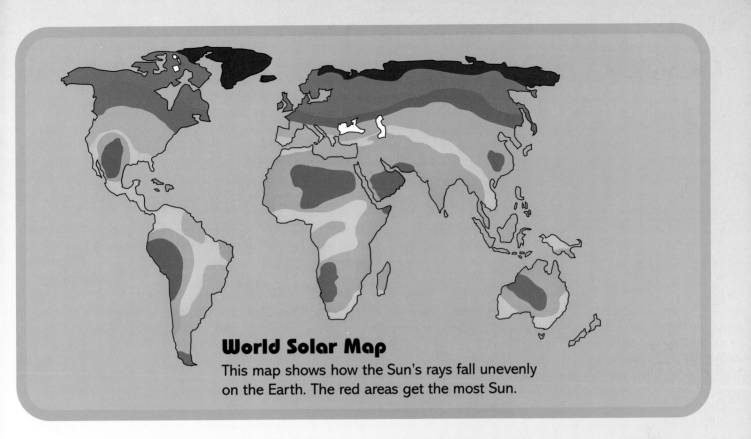

World Solar Map

This map shows how the Sun's rays fall unevenly on the Earth. The red areas get the most Sun.

Useful Websites

If you're interested in finding out more about solar power, the following websites are helpful:

www.therenewableenergycentre.co.uk
www.solarenergy.org/younger-kids
www.tonto.eia.doe.gov/kids/
www.eere.energy.gov/kids/
www.epa.gov/climatechange/kids/index.html
www.teara.govt.nz/en/wind-and-solar-
   power/3

ENERGY FACTS:
Top 10 Solar Power Nations

The ten countries with the most solar power in 2008 were (power given in megawatts):

1 **Germany** – 5,761 MW
2 **Spain** – 2,303 MW
3 **Japan** – 2,248 MW
4 **United States** – 1,407 MW
5 **India** – 413 MW
6 **China** – 256 MW
7 **Italy** – 200 MW
8 **Portugal** – 156 MW
9 **South Korea** – 139 MW
10 **France** – 89 MW

Further reading

World Issues: Energy Crisis by Ewan McLeish (Aladdin/Watts)
Our World: Solar Power by Sarah Levete (Aladdin/Watts)
Energy Sources: Solar Power by Neil Morris (Franklin Watts)
Let's Discuss Energy Resources: Solar Power by Adam Sutherland (Wayland)
Energy Debate: Solar Power by Isabel Thomas (Wayland)
Issues in Our World: Energy Crisis by Ewan McLeish (Aladdin/Watts)

Index

Photocredits

(Abbreviations: t – top, m – middle, b – bottom, l – left, r – right).

All photos istockphoto.com except: 3t, 13l: courtesy German Aerospace Center (DLR). 3b, 17tr, 17mrb, 24tr: courtesy Power Plastic®. 4-5: Concentrix Solar. 5mr: Sandia. 11l: Forwardcom/Dreamstime.com. 12r, 22tl, 25b both: Solar Millenium AG. 16tl: David Lloyd/Dreamstime.com. 16b: Suntech Power. 17tl, 20 both, 21 both: NASA. 17br: Noon Solar. 18bl: www.iea-pvps.org. 19tr: BP Angola. 19mr & br: courtesy Watercone®. 22-23: Acciona Solar Power. 25tl: Siemens AG. 25ml: US Department of Energy. 26tl: JAXA. 26b: PlanetSolar. 26mr: Büro North. 27tl: Galyna Andrushko/Dreamstime.com. 27b: courtesy Solar Sailor.